AUDITING & ASSURANCE

Dr. DAVID ACKAH

Ph.D. /M.Phil./MSc/BSc/Dip

About The Author

Dr. David Ackah was born in the Western part of Ghana, precisely Egyambra in the Ahanta West District. He had his basic and secondary education from Egyambra Basic Education, and Esiama Secondary School.

He then obtains Diploma in Economics and Business Management from Colorado Technical University, and Community College of Southern Nevada. Dr. David Ackah again continues his education to University College of Management Studies - UCOMS to read BSc Accounting, as life goes on, he had an admission to study at Atlantic International University at Hawaii precisely Honolulu in USA and Colorado Technical University to read Master of Science (MSc) and Master of Philosophy (M.Phil.) in Economics, with his hard working, he had 3.98 GPA score after his Master of Science in Economics, with this, he again obtain an admission with automatic enrolment to study Doctor of Philosophy in Economics.

Dr. Ackah also studies other professional course from the following institutions: Managing and Marketing Sales Association (MAMSA in Cherish England), Standard Diploma in Sales Management, Institute of Commercial Management (ICM in UK), Diploma in Marketing, and Institute of Export and Shipping Management (IESM in Ghana) Diploma in Marketing & Salesmanship

Dr. Ackah has work with many companies like Tobinco Pharmaceutical Ltd as Marketing Manager in Takoradi, Nutraculture Indian Pharma as Country Manager in Ghana, and Pharmanova Ltd as a Regional Marketing Manager and Teaches in many Colleges, and Secondary schools.

Currently He is a Lecturer in Kwame Nkrumah University of Science Technology, Uniworld University College, and the CEO of Regaro Group of Companies

DEDICATION

I dedicate this Book to God for his love and mecry throughout my traveling on schooling period. I again dedicate this book to my one only love Mrs Makafui Ackah, a lecturer at Accra Poly.

ACKNOWLEDGEMENT

I first and foremost express my love to God for his blessings on me every day during and after the work, and also my old school lectures for the support to me.

And also to my lovely wife Makafui Ackah for her advice and support I really appreciate it.

CHAPTER ONE
NATURE & SCOPE OF AUDITING

To assure someone can mean to comfort, convince, encourage or to persuade. It can also mean to affirm, attest or confirm. To audit means to check, examine, investigate, review, inspect or scrutinise.

In the context of companies audit and assurance can be used to scrutinise subject matter on behalf of users of that subject matter. Most importantly, auditors scrutinise financial statements on behalf of shareholders.

Audit and assurance are large topic areas. They can be further broken down into the following sub-topics:

- The scope and regulation of audit and assurance,
- Internal audit,
- Audit planning,
- Internal systems of control,
- Audit evidence,
- Audit completion, and
- Audit reports.

THE SCOPE AND REGULATION OF AUDIT AND ASSURANCE

In the context of companies audit and assurance services are provided to users of specified subject matter, upon which those users will make economic decisions. Those decisions not only affect the health and wealth of the company and the shareholders but the whole economy in which those companies are based.

The infamous liquidations of the likes of Enron and Lehman Brothers and the high profile frauds in companies such as WorldCom, Tyco International, Tragus Group and Enron have had profound and long lasting impacts on world economies, the US economy in particular.

It is therefore important that audit and assurance is carried out appropriately and competently so that the users of those services feel sufficiently confident to make their decisions. Since the frauds mentioned above the assurance profession has, sadly but rightly, suffered from a loss of trust. In response global regulators have adopted new forms
of regulation and governance and introduced new standards of performance in an attempt to win that trust back.

ACCEPTING AUDIT ENGAGEMENTS

Preconditions for an audit

Auditors should only accept a new audit engagement, or continue an existing audit engagement if the 'preconditions for an audit' required by ISA 210 Agreeing the terms of audit engagements are present.

ISA 210 requires the auditor to:

- Determine whether the financial reporting framework to be applied in the preparation of the financial statements is appropriate; and
- Obtain the agreement of management that it acknowledges and understands its responsibilities.

4

If the preconditions for an audit are not present, the auditor should discuss the matter with management, and should not accept the engagement unless required to do so by law or regulation.

Procedures

If offered an audit role, the auditor should:

- Ask the client for permission to contact the outgoing auditor (reject role if client refuses)
- Contact the outgoing auditor, asking for any reasons why they should not accept appointment. If a reply is not received, the prospective auditor should try and contact the outgoing auditor by other means e.g. by telephone. If a reply is still not received the prospective auditor may still choose to accept but must proceed with care.
- Ensure that the legal requirements in relation to the removal of the previous auditors and the appointment of the firm have been met
- Carry out checks to ensure the firm can be independent, is competent to do this audit and has the necessary resources
- Assess whether this work is suitably low risk
- Assess the integrity of the company's directors
- As a commercial organisation, the firm should also ensure that this is a desirable client (e.g. right industry, suitable profit margin etc)
- Not accept the appointment, where it is known that a limitation will be placed on the scope of the audit.

Engagement letters

The engagement letter will be sent before the audit. It specifies the nature of the contract between the audit firm and the client and minimises the risk of any misunderstanding of the auditor's role.

It should be reviewed every year to ensure that it is up to date but does not need to be reissued every year unless there are changes to the terms of the engagement. The auditor must issue a new engagement letter if the scope or context of the assignment changes after initial appointment.

ISA 210 requires the auditor to consider whether there is a need to remind the entity of the existing terms of the audit engagement for recurring audits and many firms choose to send a new letter every year, to emphasise its importance to clients.

THE CONTENTS OF THE ENGAGEMENT LETTER

The contents of a letter of engagement for audit services are listed in **ISA 210** Agreeing the Terms of Audit Engagements. They should include the following:

- The objective and scope of the audit;
- The responsibilities of the auditor;
- The responsibilities of management;
- The identification of an applicable financial reporting framework; and
- Reference to the expected form and content of any reports to be issued.

In addition to the above the engagement letter may also make reference to:
- The unavoidable risk that some material misstatements may go undetected due to the inherent limitations in an audit;
- Arrangements regarding the planning and performance of the audit;
- The expectation that management will provide written representations;
- The agreement of management to make available to the auditor draft financial statements and other information in time to complete the audit in accordance with the proposed timetable;
- The agreement of management to inform the auditor of facts that may affect the financial statements;
- The basis on which fees are computed and billing arrangements;
- A request for management to acknowledge receipt of the engagement letter and to agree the terms outlined;
- Agreements concerning the involvement of auditors experts and internal auditors; and
- Restrictions to the auditor's liability.

ASSURANCE

"An engagement in which a practitioner expresses a conclusion designed to enhance the degree of confidence of the intended users about the outcome of the evaluation or measurement of a subject matter against criteria."

In simple terms, giving assurance means: offering an opinion about specific information so the users of that information are able to make **confident decisions** knowing that the **risk** of the information being 'incorrect' is **reduced**.

THE ELEMENTS OF AN ASSURANCE ENGAGEMENT

There are **5 elements** of an assurance engagement:
- The three parties involved:
    - ♣ The practitioner (i.e. the reviewer of the information);
    - ♣ The intended users (of the information); and
    - ♣ The responsible party (i.e. the preparer of the information).
- The subject matter under scrutiny;
- Suitable criteria against which to judge the reliability and accuracy of the subject matter (e.g. IFRS);
- Sufficient appropriate evidence to substantiate an opinion; and
- A written report in an appropriate form.

Examples of assurance services
- An audit of financial statements
- A review of financial statements
- Risk assessment reports
- Systems reliability reports

- Reports on social and environmental issues (e.g. to validate an employer's claims about being an equal opportunities employer or a company's claims about sustainable sourcing of materials)
- Reviews of internal controls
- Value for money audit in public sector organisations.

TYPES OF ASSURANCE ENGAGEMENT

The IAASB International Framework for Assurance Engagements permits two types of assurance engagement:

- Reasonable, and
- Limited.

Reasonable assurance engagements

In a reasonable assurance engagement, the practitioner:

- Gathers **sufficient appropriate evidence** to be able to draw reasonable conclusions;
- Concludes that the subject matter conforms in **all material respects** with identified suitable criteria; and
- Gives a **positively** worded assurance opinion.

Illustration of a positively worded assurance opinion

"In our opinion, the financial statements present fairly, in all material respects (or give a true and fair view of) the financial position of ABC Company as at December 31 20X1, and (*of*) its financial performance and its cash flows for the year then ended in accordance with International Financial Reporting Standards."

Statutory audit is an example of a reasonable assurance assignment. The approach to these assignments must be consistent with local legislative requirements, such as the Companies Act in the UK, and audit work will need to be carried out in accordance with International Standards on Auditing (ISAs).

LIMITED ASSURANCE ENGAGEMENT

In a limited assurance assignment the practitioner:

- Gathers **sufficient appropriate evidence** to be able to draw limited conclusions;
- Concludes that the subject matter, with respect to identified suitable criteria, **is plausible in the circumstances**; and
- Gives a **negatively** worded assurance opinion.

Illustration of a negatively worded assurance opinion

"Nothing has come to our attention that causes us to believe that the financial statements as of 31 December 2011 are not prepared, in all material respects, in accordance with an applicable financial reporting framework."

An example of a limited assurance assignment is a **review engagement**. It is possible for small companies, who are not legally required to have a full audit, to have a review of their financial statements to enable them to present their accounts to potential lenders.

There is no precise definition of what is meant by reasonable or limited in this context. However, it is clear that the confidence inspired by a reasonable assurance report is designed to be greater than that inspired by a limited one.
It therefore follows that:

- There are more regulations/standards governing a reasonable assurance assignment;
- The procedures carried out in a reasonable assurance assignment will be more thorough; and
- The evidence gathered in a reasonable assurance assignment will need to be of a higher quality.

REVIEW ENGAGEMENTS

The **objective of a review of financial statements** is to enable an auditor to state whether, on the basis of procedures which do not provide all the evidence required in an audit, anything has come to the auditor's attention that causes the auditor to believe that the financial statements are not prepared in accordance with the applicable financial reporting framework (ie negative/limited assurance).

Guidance on how to perform this type of assignment is given by the IAASB in International Standard on Review Engagements (ISRE) 2400, Engagements to Review Financial Statements.

CHARACTERISTICS

Review engagements will be carried out using much more limited procedures than a statutory audit. Typically the following procedures are used:

- analytical review; and
- enquiry

THE EXPECTATIONS GAP

The greatest level of assurance auditors can provide is reasonable. The limitations of an audit mean that **it is not possible to provide 'absolute' assurance**. These limitations include:

- Financial information includes subjective and judgemental matters.
- Inherent limitations of controls used as audit evidence.
- Representations from management may have to be relied upon as the only source of evidence in some areas.
- Evidence is often persuasive not conclusive; and auditors
- Do not review 100% of the transactions and balances; they test on a sample basis.

Some users incorrectly believe that an audit does provide absolute assurance; that the audit opinion is a guarantee the financial statements are 'correct'. This and other misconceptions about the role an auditor plays are often referred to as the **'Expectations Gap.'** Other examples of these misconceptions include:

- A belief that auditors test 100% of transactions and balances: they test on a sample basis;
- A belief that auditors are required to detect fraud; auditors are required to offer an opinion that the financial statements are free from material misstatement, which may be caused by fraud;

- Auditors are responsible for preparing the financial statements; this is the responsibility of management.

AUDIT ENGAGEMENTS

In most developed countries, publicly listed companies and large companies are required by law to produce annual financial statements and have them audited by an independent, external auditor.

Other organisations (e.g. small private companies, partnerships, etc.) may choose to be audited even if there is no legal requirement.

THE OBJECTIVE OF AN AUDIT

The objective of an external audit engagement is to enable the auditor to express an opinion on whether the financial statements

- Give a true and fair view (or present fairly in all material respects), and
- Are prepared, in all material respects, in accordance with an applicable financial reporting framework.

The financial reporting framework to be applied will vary from country to country.

GENERAL PRINCIPLES

The auditor should follow certain general principles in the conduct of an external audit.

- Compliance with applicable ethical principles, i.e. the IFAC Code of Ethics for Professional Accountants and the ethical pronouncements of the auditor's professional body, e.g. the ACCA's Rules of Professional Conduct.
- Compliance with applicable auditing standards, i.e. the International Auditing and Assurance Standards Board's (IAASB's) International Standards on Auditing (ISAs).
- Planning and performing the audit with an attitude of professional scepticism that recognises that the financial statements being audited may be materially misstated.
- Relevant national legal frameworks.

REGULATION OF AUDIT AND ASSURANCE

The need for regulation

The role of the auditor has come under increased scrutiny over the last thirty years due to an increase in high profile, economically damaging fraud cases. The most high profile case, and the catalyst for regulatory change, was the collapse of Enron and its auditor Arthur Andersen. In order to try and regain trust in the auditing profession national and international standard setters and regulators have tried to introduce three initiatives:

- Harmonisation of auditing procedures, so that users of audit services are confident in the nature of audits being conducted around the world;
- A focus on audit quality, so that the expectations of users are met; and
- Adherence to a strict ethical code of conduct, to try and improve the perception of auditors as independent, unbiased service providers.

In order to achieve this practitioners now have to follow three sets of regulatory guidance:

- The Code of Ethics for Professional Accountants
- Auditing Standards, particularly International Standards on Auditing, and

- National corporate law including regulations regarding corporate governance.

FRAUDULENT BEHAVIOUR

Introduction

Fraud can be defined as an intentional deception designed for either personal gain. Fraudulent behaviour constitutes criminal activity and can lead to significant consequences, including imprisonment.

There are many types of fraudulent behaviour connected to companies. They include:

- Insider dealing and market abuse
- Money laundering
- Bribery
- Fraudulent and wrongful trading, and
- General criminal activity in the management of a company

Criminal Activity in the Management of Companies

There are a number of criminal offences that could be undertaken by individuals concerned in the operation, management or winding up of a company.

Failure to File Accounts or Annual R Returns

Failure to deliver accounts or annual returns on time is a criminal offence. All the directors of a company in default could be prosecuted. If convicted, a director could end up with a criminal record and a fine of up to £5,000 for each offence.

Providing Misleading Information to an Auditor

Under s499 CA 2006, an auditor is entitled to require from the company's officers and employees such information and explanation as he thinks necessary for the performance of his duties as auditor. It is a criminal offence for an officer of the company to:

- Provide misleading, false or deceptive information or explanations, or
- Fail to provide information or explanations required by the auditor.

An individual can defend such as charge if he can prove that it was not reasonably practicable to provide the information or explanations required.

Business Name

Under Section 82 Companies Act 2006 it is a criminal offence to use a business name that requires prior approval, if that approval has not been obtained.

It is also a criminal offence to fail to disclose the business details that the Act requires. These details include stating the company's corporate name and address for the service of documents.

Company Directors Disqualification Act 1986 (CDDA 1986)

Under s13 CDDA 1986, any person who acts in contravention of a disqualification order (or while an undercharged bankrupt) is guilty of an offence. The maximum penalty is:

- Two years' imprisonment and/or a fine on conviction on indictment

- Up to six months' imprisonment and/or a fine not exceeding the statutory maximum on a summary conviction.

S15 CDDA 1986 provides that anyone who is involved in the management of a company while disqualified, or who acts on the instructions of someone who is disqualified, shall be personally liable for the company's debts incurred during the time they acted.

Phoenix companies

S216 and s217 Insolvency Act 1986 (IA 1986) are aimed at so-called 'phoenix companies'. They apply where a person was a director or shadow director of a company at any time in the period of 12 months ending with the day before the company went into liquidation.

The provisions apply for the five years following liquidation. They prevent the person being a director of a company with a similar name, or a name which suggests an association with the previous company, without leave of the court.

It is a criminal offence to contravene the provisions, punishable by imprisonment and/or a fine. In addition, the director will be personally liable for any debts of the new company which are incurred when he was involved in its management.

The Fraud Act 2006

The Fraud Act 2006 radically changed the law of criminal fraud.

Before the Fraud Act came into force, the statutory fraud offences under the Theft Act 1978 were based on deception. They included:

- Obtaining property by deception.
- Obtaining a money transfer by deception.
- Obtaining a pecuniary advantage by deception.
- Obtaining services by deception.

The Fraud Act swept all of the old statutory deception offences away. Instead a new offence of fraud has been defined as follows:

The defendant must have been dishonest, and have intended to make a gain or to cause a loss to another; and the defendant must carry out one of these acts:

- Making a false or misleading representation, this being where any person makes "any representation as to fact or law ... express or implied" which they know to be untrue or misleading
- Failing to disclose information whereby a person fails to disclose any information to a third party when they are under a legal duty to disclose such information
- Abuse of position where a person occupies a position where they are expected to safeguard the financial interests of another person, and abuses that position; this includes cases where the abuse consisted of an omission rather than an overt act.

The new offence of fraud is intended to be wide and also flexible. There is no reliance on the concept of "deception". It does not matter whether the false information actually deceives anyone; it is the misleading intention which counts.

CHAPTER TWO
INTERNAL SYSTEM OF CONTROL

Corporate governance is the system by which a company is directed and controlled. The directors, or management, of a company are those individuals responsible for this.

As stewards of a company (i.e. they run the company on behalf of the owners), directors are responsible: for making operational decisions in the best interests of the owners; safeguarding the assets of the owners; and providing the owners with relevant and timely information that they can use to assist with their decision making.

One of the key components of this is the need to implement internal control systems. They are vital to the effective operation of the company.

There are of particular significance to and auditor because the strength of a client's internal controls directly impacts the risk of:

- Non-compliance with laws and regulations,
- Fraud, and
- Misstatement in the financial reporting system.

Auditors therefore have to gain an understanding of the strengths and deficiencies of the system to assist their risk assessment during the planning process. This includes:

- Understanding the components of the internal system of control,
- Documenting and testing the system, and
- Identifying and reporting deficiencies in the system.

DOCUMENTING AND TESTING CONTROL SYSTEMS
Ascertaining How the System Operates

Procedures used to obtain evidence regarding the design and implementation of controls include

- Enquiries of relevant personnel;
- Observing the application of controls;
- Tracing transactions through systems; and
- Inspecting documents, such as internal procedure manuals.

In addition to this, auditors can also use their prior knowledge of the client and the operation of the systems in prior years. However, it must be noted, that auditors cannot simply rely on their systems knowledge from the prior year's audit; much can happen in a year and systems knowledge must be updated and the systems tested once more.

It should also be noted that ISA 315 specifies that enquiry, alone, is not sufficient to understand the nature and extent of controls.

Documenting client systems

Possible ways of documenting systems include:

- Narrative notes (which can prove bulky if systems are large or complex)
- Flowcharts (which can make a complex system easier to follow)
- Organisation charts - showing roles, responsibilities, and reporting lines
- Internal Control Questionnaire (**ICQ**)
- Internal Control Evaluation Questionnaire (**ICE**).

ISA 315 states that the method adopted is a matter of auditor judgement.

ICQs

An **ICQ** is a list of possible controls for each area of the Financial Statements. The client is asked to review the list and confirm which are applicable to their system.

ICEs

In contrast to ICQ's an **ICE** lists control objectives. Clients are then asked to confirm how they meet that objective.

For example; an ICQ might ask a client: "does a supervisor authorise all weekly timesheets?" An ICE would ask "how does the company ensure that only hours worked are recorded on timesheets?"

Testing the system

Having documented the systems the auditor needs to assess whether:

- They are actually implemented; and
- They are effective.

In order to assess the operating effectiveness of controls in preventing and detecting material misstatement the auditor performs tests of controls. These are designed to gather evidence concerning:

- How controls were applied during the period;
- The consistency of application; and
- Who (or what) they were applied by.

Typical methods of controls testing include:

- Walkthrough tests, where a transaction is followed through the system;
- Observation of control activities, e.g. the inventory count; and
- Computer aided audit techniques (as seen in the audit evidence chapter).

REPORTING DEFICIENCIES IN INTERNAL CONTROL SYSTEMS

Auditors should communicate deficiencies in internal control identified during the course of an audit to those charged with governance and management. In particular, significant deficiencies should be communicated in writing to those charged with governance. This is a requirement of **ISA 265** Communicating Deficiencies in Internal Control to Those Charged with Governance and Management.

The form, timing and addressees of this communication should be agreed at the start of the audit, as part of the terms of the engagement. This report, traditionally known as a management letter or report to management is usually sent at the end of the audit process. When the auditor reports deficiencies, it should be made clear that:

- The report is not a comprehensive list of deficiencies, but only those that have come to light during normal audit procedures
- The report is for the sole use of the company
- No disclosure should be made to a third party without the written agreement of the auditor
- No responsibility is assumed to any other parties.

THE COMPONENTS OF AN INTERNAL CONTROL SYSTEM

ISA 315 Identifying and Assessing the Risks of Material Misstatement Through Understanding the Entity and its Environment states that auditors need to understand an entity's internal controls. To assist this process it identifies five components of an internal control system:

- The control environment;
- The entity's risk assessment process;
- The information system;
- The control activities; and
- The monitoring of controls.

The control environment

The control environment includes the governance and management function of an organisation. It focuses largely on the attitude, awareness and actions of those responsible for designing, implementing and monitoring internal controls. Elements of the control environment that are relevant when the auditor obtains an understanding include the following:

- Communication and enforcement of integrity and ethical values;
- Commitment to competence;
- participation by those charged with governance;
- Management's philosophy and operating style;
- Organisational structure;
- Assignment of authority and responsibility; and
- Human resource policies and practices.

Evidence regarding the control environment is usually obtained through a mixture of enquiry and observation, although inspection of key internal documents (e.g. codes of conduct and organisation charts) is possible.

The risk assessment process

The risk assessment process forms the basis for how management determines the risks to be managed. These processes will vary hugely depending upon the nature, size and complexity of the organisation. However, larger organisations (usually listed ones) will have internal audit departments, whose roles focus heavily on risk identification and assessment.
If the client has robust procedures for assessing the business risks it faces, the risk of misstatement, overall, will be lower.

The information system

The information systems relevant to financial reporting objectives include all the procedures and records which are designed to:

- Initiate, record, process and report transactions;
- Maintain accountability for assets, liabilities and equity;
- Resolve incorrect processing of transactions;
- Process and account for system overrides;
- Transfer information to the general/nominal ledger;

- Capture information relevant to financial reporting for other events and conditions; and
- Ensure information required to be disclosed is appropriately reported.

Control activities

The control activities include all policies and procedures designed to ensure that management directives are carried out throughout the organisation. Examples of specific control activities include those relating to:

- Authorisation;
- Performance review;
- Information processing;
- Physical controls; and
- Segregation of duties.

IT affects the way in which control activities are implemented. It is important that auditors assess how controls over IT maintain the integrity and security of information held on them. Such controls are normally divided into two categories:

- Application; and
- General.

Application controls

Application controls are either manual or automated and typically operate at the business process level and apply to the processing of transactions. Examples include:

- Batch total checks;
- Sequence checks;
- Matching master files to transaction records;
- Arithmetic checks;
- Range checks (to ensure that data stays within reasonable ranges);
- Existence checks (e.g. to check employees exist);
- Authorisation of transaction entries
- Exception reporting

An example is that Quickbooks, a small business accounting package, will not let you enter a sale until you have set up an 'item', which means you have to allocate the sale to a revenue account, set up the customer as a receivable, decide on VAT treatment, etc.

General controls

General IT controls are policies and procedures that relate to many applications and support the effective functioning of application controls by helping to ensure the continued proper operation of information systems, e.g. controls over:

- Data centre and network operations
- System software acquisition
- Program change and maintenance
- Access security - passwords, door locks, swipe cards
- Backup procedures.

A healthy IT system should include both application and general control procedures.

Monitoring of controls

This is the process of assessing the effectiveness of controls over time and taking necessary remedial action. Clearly if a control is not implemented properly or is simply considered ineffective then misstatements may pass undetected into the financial statements. Monitoring can be either on-going or performed on a separate evaluation basis (or a combination of both). Either way, it needs to be effective for the system to work. Monitoring of internal controls is often the key role of internal auditors.

CHAPTER THREE
INTERNAL AUDIT

Internal Audit

Definition

"The role of internal audit is to provide independent assurance that an organisation's risk management, governance and internal control processes are operating effectively. Internal auditors deal with issues that are fundamentally important to the survival and prosperity of any organisation. Unlike external auditors, they look beyond financial risks and statements to consider wider issues such as the organisation's reputation, growth, its impact on the environment and the way it treats its employees." (Chartered Institute of Internal Auditors)

The difference between internal and external audit

Internal auditors are often confused with external auditors, but there are significant differences between the two groups. Internal auditors look at all the risks facing an organisation and what is being done to manage these risks. External auditors on the other hand look at financial accounts. So internal audit's role is broader and might, for example, include auditing the reputational risk that a company could be damaged by using cheap labour in foreign countries. It could also include auditing operational risks such as poor health and safety procedures, or strategic risks such as the board stretching company resources by producing too many products. (Chartered Institute of Internal Auditors)

Regulatory guidance

The UK Corporate Governance Code

This sets out the requirements relating to the composition and functions of the audit committee (or equivalent body). As a minimum, they must:

- monitor the financial reporting process;
- monitor the effectiveness of the company's internal control, internal audit, and risk management systems.

Where there is no internal audit function, the audit committee should consider annually whether there is a need for an internal audit function and make a recommendation to the board.

Where there is no internal audit function, the reasons for the absence of such a function should be explained in the relevant section of the annual report

The Sarbanes-Oxley Act (2002) (US)

Section 404 of the Act requires companies to document, evaluate, test and monitor their internal controls over financial reporting. This requires the senior management of a company to assess the design, operating effectiveness and adequacy of internal controls over financial reporting. Management often turns to internal audit to support compliance with these requirements.

Management are required to issue an annual report that addresses any material deficiencies in the company's internal controls. Section 404 also requires that the external auditor attests to assertions made by management about the effectiveness of the systems and controls.

The scope of the internal audit function

The role of internal audit can be much more varied than that of an external auditor depending on the requirements of the business. Typically they provide assurance to internal management on issues such as:

- The effectiveness of systems (financial, legal and operational);
- The effectiveness of internal controls;
- Whether company procedures/manuals are being followed
- Whether internally produced information is reliable; and
- Whether the company is compliant with relevant corporate governance requirements.

In addition to the above, internal audit will carry out ad hoc assignments, as required by management, e.g.: internal fraud investigations.

Internal Audit Effectiveness

If the internal audit department is to be effective in providing assurance it needs to be:

- Sufficiently resourced, both financially and in terms of qualified, experienced staff;
- Well organised, so that it has well developed work practices; and
- Independent and objective.

This last point needs some explanation. Internal auditors are (generally) employed by the company they are reporting on and are often managed as part of the finance function. They will therefore have to report upon the effectiveness of financial systems that they form a part of. It is therefore difficult for internal audit to remain truly objective. However, acceptable levels of independence can be achieved through one, or more, of the following strategies:

- Reporting channels separate from the management of the main financial reporting function, such as an audit committee;
- Reviews of internal audit work by managers independent of the function under scrutiny; and
- Outsourcing the internal audit function to a professional third party.

LIMITATIONS OF THE INTERNAL AUDIT FUNCTION

Reporting system

The chief internal auditor reports to the finance director. This limits the effectiveness of the internal audit reports as the finance director will also be responsible for some of the financial systems that the internal auditor is reporting on. Similarly, the chief internal auditor may soften or limit criticism in reports to avoid confrontation with the finance director.

To ensure independence, the internal audit should report to an audit committee.

Scope of Work

The scope of work of internal audit is decided by the finance director in discussion with the chief internal auditor. This means that the finance director may try and influence the chief internal auditor regarding the areas that the internal audit department is auditing, possibly directing attention away from any contentious areas that the director does not want auditing.

To ensure independence, the scope of work of the internal audit department should be decided by the chief internal auditor, perhaps with the assistance of an audit committee.

Audit Work

The chief internal auditor may audit their own work. This limits independence as the auditor is effectively auditing their own work, and may not therefore identify any mistakes. This is known as self-review threat.

To ensure independence, the chief internal auditor should not establish control systems in the company. However, where controls have already been established, another member of internal audit should carry out the audit of that system to provide some limited independence.

Lengths of Service of Internal Audit Staff

Internal audit staff may be employed for a long period of time. This may limit their effectiveness as they will be very familiar with the systems being reviewed and therefore may not be sufficiently objective to identify errors in those systems.

To ensure independence, the existing staff should be rotated into different areas of internal audit work and the chief internal auditor should independently review the work carried out.

Appointment of Chief Internal Auditor

The chief internal auditor is appointed by an executive director/CEO. Given that the CEO is responsible for the running of the company, it is possible that there will be bias in the appointment of the chief internal auditor; the CEO may appoint someone who he knows will not criticise his work or the company.

To ensure independence, the chief internal auditor should be appointed by an audit committee or at least the appointment agreed by the whole board.

Variation of standards

Standards of audit are not uniform across the profession. This could lead to inconsistency in the way internal audit is performed (both on a year-to-year basis and amongst different companies) and it can lead to manipulation of internal audit aims and measurement criteria by companies.

Outsourcing the Internal Audit Function

In common with other areas of a company's operations, the directors may consider that outsourcing the internal audit function represents better value than an in-house provision. Local government authorities are under particular pressure to ensure that all their services represent 'best value' and this may prompt them to decide to adopt a competitive tender approach.

Advantages

- Greater focus on cost and efficiency of the internal audit function.
- Staff may be drawn from a broader range of expertise.
- Risk of staff turnover is passed to the outsourcing firm.
- Specialist skills may be more readily available.
- Costs of employing permanent staff are avoided.
- May improve independence.

- Access to new market place technologies, e.g. audit methodology software without associated costs.
- Reduced management time in administering an in-house department.

Disadvantages
- Possible conflict of interest if provided by the external auditors (In some jurisdictions, e.g. the UK, the ethics rules specifically prohibit the external auditors from providing internal audit services).
- Pressure on the independence of the outsourced function due to, e.g. threat by management not to renew contract.
- Risk of lack of knowledge and understanding of the organisation's objectives, culture or business.
- The decision may be based on cost with the effectiveness of the function being reduced.
- Flexibility and availability may not be as high as with an in-house function.
- Lack of control over standard of service.
- Risk of blurring of roles between internal and external audit, losing credibility for both.

Internal audit assignments
Internal auditors perform many different types of assignment. Common examples include:
Value for money

Value for money (VFM) is concerned with obtaining the best possible combination of services for the least resources. It is often referred to as a review of the three "E's":
- **Economy:** obtaining the best quality of resources for the minimum cost;
- **Efficiency:** obtaining the maximum departmental/organisational outputs with the minimum use of resources; and
- **Effectiveness:** achievement of goals and targets (departmental/organisational etc).

Comparisons of value for money achieved by different organisations (or branches of the same organisation) are often made using performance indicators that provide a measure of economy, efficiency or effectiveness. This is particularly common in the 'not-for-profit' sector (i.e. public services and charities)

The audit of IT systems
The external auditor considers IT systems from the perspective of whether they provide a reliable basis for the preparation of financial statements, and whether there are internal controls which are effective in reducing the risk of misstatement.
Internal audit will also consider this. However, their role is much wider in scope and will also consider whether:
- The company is getting value for money;
- The procurement process was effective; and
- The on-going management/maintenance of the system is appropriate.

Whilst this is an on-going role project auditing can be used to look at whether the objectives of a specific project, such as commissioning a new factory or implementing new IT systems, were achieved.

Financial Audit

The main aim of a financial reporting system, from a business' perspective; is to create accurate, complete and timely information to be used as a basis for internal decision making and business planning. This information is also needed to satisfy the requirements of actual and potential investors and trading partners.

Typical examples of financial information include:

- Annual financial statements;
- Interim financial statements;
- Monthly management accounts; and
- Forecasts and projections,

The main aim of internal financial audit is to ensure that the information produced is reliable and produced in an efficient timely manner. If not then executive decisions may be based upon unreliable information or, may not be possible at all.

The other aim of financial audit is to assess the financial health of a business. More importantly it is about ensuring there are mechanisms in place for the early identification of financial risk, such as:

- Adverse currency fluctuations;
- Adverse interest rate fluctuations; and
- Inflation.

In both cases the focus of internal audit will be on the processes and controls that underpin the creation of the various financial reports to ensure that they are as effective as possible for assisting the various decisions and risk management processes of the company.
Operational internal audit assignments

Operational auditing covers:

- Examination and review of the whole, or part of, a business' operations;
- The effectiveness of operational controls; and
- Identification of areas for improvement in efficiency and performance.

In operational audit a risk based approach should be used that:

- Identifies the principal business risks involved which may prevent the organisation achieving its objectives; and
- Assesses the extent to which controls are in place and are operating effectively in order to manage these risks.

The outcome of each assignment should be a report to management which appraises the control systems which are currently in place and which makes appropriate recommendations for improvement

CHAPTER FOUR
AUDIT PLANNING

Auditing is regulated more now than ever before. Due to high profile fraud cases, such as Enron, auditors are constantly in the spotlight. The consequences of performing a poor or, even worse, a negligent audit could be severe in terms of both damage to reputation and possible litigation. It is therefore vital that auditors have an appropriate system of quality control to ensure that they perform their engagements effectively.

One of the elements of a good quality control in an audit is planning. The main elements the planning process include devising and audit strategy and an audit plan, the aims of which are to reduce audit risk.

In addition auditors must consider their responsibilities with regard to fraud and laws and regulations.

THE AUDIT PLANNING PROCESS

Planning Objectives

"The objective of the auditor is to plan the audit so that it will be performed in an effective manner." (**ISA 300** Planning and Audit of Financial Statements).

Audits are potentially complex, risky and expensive processes for an accountancy firm. Although firms have internal manuals and standardised procedures it is vital that engagements are planned to ensure that the auditor:

- Devotes appropriate attention to important areas of the audit;
- Identifies and resolves potential problems on a timely basis;
- Organises and manages the audit so that it is performed in an effective and efficient manner;
- Selects team members with appropriate capabilities and competencies;
- Directs and supervises the team and reviews their work; and
- Effectively coordinates the work of others, such as experts and internal audit.

The purpose of all this is to ensure that the risk of performing a poor quality audit (and ultimately giving an inappropriate audit opinion) is reduced to an acceptable level.

The planning process

Planning consists of a number of elements. However, they could be summarised as:

Preliminary engagement activities:

- Evaluating compliance with ethical requirements; and
- Establishing the terms of the engagement.

Planning activities:

- Developing the audit strategy; and
- Developing an audit plan.

AUDIT STRATEGY

Introduction
The audit strategy sets the scope, timing and direction of the audit. It allows the auditor to determine the following:

- The resources to deploy for specific audit areas (e.g. experience level, external experts);
- The amount of resources to allocate (e.g. number of team members);
- When the resources are to be deployed; and
- How the resources are managed, directed and supervised, including the timings of meetings debriefs and reviews.

Considerations in Establishing the Overall Strategy
In determining the audit strategy the auditor should:

- Identify the characteristics of the engagement;
- Ascertain the reporting objectives to plan the timing of the audit and the nature of communications;
- Consider the significant factors that will direct the team's efforts;
- Consider the results of preliminary engagement activities; and
- Ascertain the nature, timing and extent of resources necessary to perform the engagement.

Characteristics of the Engagement
- What is the financial reporting framework for the financial statements?
- Are there industry specific requirements? e.g. listed companies and charities;
- The number and locations of premises, branches, subsidiaries etc;
- The nature of the client and the need for specialised knowledge;
- The reporting currency;
- The effect of IT on audit procedures, including availability of data.

Reporting objectives, timing of the audit, and nature of communication
- The timetable for interim and final reporting;
- The organisation of meetings with management;
- The expected types and timings of auditor's reports/communications;
- The expected nature and timing of communication amongst team members; and
- Whether there are any expected communications with third parties.

Significant factors and preliminary engagement activities
- Materiality;
- Results of risk assessment;
- Professional scepticism;
- Results of previous audits;
- Evidence of management's commitment to internal controls;
- Volume of transactions;
- Significant business developments/changes;

- Significant industry developments; and
- Significant financial reporting changes.

Nature, timing and extent of resources
- The selection of and assignment of work to the engagement team; and
- Budgets.

ANALYTICAL PROCEDURES

Definition

Analytical procedures are fundamental to the auditing process and are used at the planning, performance and review stage of the audit. They are defined in **ISA 520** Analytical Procedures as:

"The evaluation of financial information through analysis of plausible relationships among both financial and non-financial data."

Methods and uses

Traditionally they incorporate the comparison of:
- Current and prior year figures;
- Current and budgeted/forecast figures; and
- Client and industry average figures.

At the planning stage analytical procedures are useful for helping to gain an understanding of the client's performance over the last twelve months and to identify any significant changes to the business, for example: the disposal of significant land and buildings. In addition, analytical procedures are also used to identify peculiar deviations (from either prior year figures, budget or the auditor's knowledge) that could indicate misstatement in the reported figures. These must then be investigated during final audit procedures.

For example; when conducting an analytical review of a current audit client you notice that turnover had increased by 20% in comparison to last year but delivery costs have increased by 50%. Normally you would expect costs to rise in line with changes in activity but clearly delivery costs have increased at a much higher rate. Plausible reasons for this variance include:

- Increasing sales by attracting customers from more distant geographical locations;
- Reducing delivery waiting times by making more frequent deliveries; or
- There is an error in either sales or delivery costs.

The reason for the variance will be investigated during the audit until a satisfactory explanation is obtained.

MATERIALITY

Definition

Materiality is a concept, a threshold, an intangible. What makes misstatement material to one user of the accounts may not be material to another user. The precise definition is as follows: "Misstatements, including omissions, are considered to be material if they, individually or in the aggregate, could reasonably be expected to influence the economic decisions of users taken on the basis of the financial statements" (**ISA 320** Materiality in Planning and Performing an Audit)

The Significance of Materiality

The bottom line is that the auditor is responsible for providing an opinion on whether the financial statements are prepared, in all **material** respects, in accordance with an applicable financial reporting framework. If financial statements contain material misstatement they cannot be deemed to show a true and fair view and are therefore an unreliable basis for users' decision making.

As a result the focus of an audit is identifying the significant risks of material misstatement in the financial statements and then designing procedures aimed at identifying and quantifying material misstatement.

Determining Materiality

The most significant misunderstanding about materiality is that it is a purely financial concern. However, disclosures in the financial statements pertaining to possible future legal claims, for example, could influence users' decisions and may be purely narrative. In this case a numerical calculation is not relevant.

The guidance in ISA 320 states that the determination of materiality is a matter of professional judgement and that the auditor must consider:

- The circumstances surrounding the entity;
- Both the size and nature of misstatements; and
- The information needs of the users as a group.

This is an obviously subjective and potentially complex process but is vital in ensuring that materiality is considered in light of the client's needs, instead of just applying an arbitrary calculation. However, ISA 320 does recognise the need to establish a financial threshold to guide audit planning and procedures. For this reason it does allow the use of standard benchmarks but only as a starting point. The auditor must then consider all the factors listed above. Traditional benchmarks include:

- ½ - 1% of turnover
- 5 - 10% of profit before tax
- 1 - 2% of gross assets

The Practical Application of Materiality

It is unlikely, in practice, that auditors will be able to design tests that identify individually material misstatements. It is much more common that misstatements in aggregate (i.e. in combination) become material. Auditors also have to consider that they can only test on a sample basis, so they have to evaluate their findings and determine how likely it is that errors identified in the sample are representative of material errors in the whole population under scrutiny.

For this reason materiality, as determined for the financial statements as a whole, may not be the best guide in determining the nature and extent of audit tests. To this end ISA's introduce two further concepts: performance materiality and tolerable misstatement that guide the way an auditor performs, and evaluates the results of, their tests.

Performance Materiality

This is defined in ISA 320 as:

"The amount set by the auditor at less than materiality for the financial statements as a whole to reduce to an appropriately low level the probability that the aggregate of uncorrected and undetected misstatements exceeds materiality for the financial statements as a whole."

In using this lower threshold to perform audit procedures the auditor is more likely to identify misstatements, the effect of which can be considered in combination.

Tolerable Misstatement

This is defined in **ISA 530** Audit Sampling as:

"A monetary amount set by the auditor in respect of which the auditor seeks to obtain an appropriate level of assurance that the monetary amount set by the auditor is not exceeded by the actual misstatement in the population."

It is the practical application of performance materiality to an audit sample. If the total of errors in the sample selected exceeds tolerable misstatement the auditor considers that the risk of a material misstatement from the whole population is high and therefore tests a greater sample size. If the total of errors in the sample is less than tolerable misstatement then the auditor may be reasonably confident that the risk of material misstatement in the whole population is low and no further testing will be required.

RISK ASSESSMENT

Introduction

Auditors are required to assess audit risk and reduce it to an acceptably low level. In conducting a thorough assessment of risk auditors will be able to:

- Identify areas of the financial statements where misstatements are likely to occur;
- Plan procedures that address the significant risk areas identified;
- Carry out an efficient, focussed and effective audit;
- Minimise the risk of issuing an inappropriate audit opinion to an acceptable level;
- Reduce the risk of reputational and punitive damage.

Although risk assessment is a fundamental element of the planning process, it is important to understand that risks can be uncovered at any stage of the audit and that procedures must be adapted in light of revelations that indicate further risks of material misstatement. It is, ultimately, the responsibility of the most senior reviewer (usually the engagement partner) to confirm that the risk of material misstatement has been reduced to an acceptable level.

Understanding the Entity and its Environment

The first stage in the risk assessment processes it to consider the risks of material misstatements in the client's financial statements in accordance with **ISA 315** Identifying and Assessing the Risks of Material Misstatement through Understanding the Entity and its Environment. These states:

'The objective of the auditor is to identify and assess the risk of material misstatement, whether due to fraud or error, at the financial statement and assertion levels, through understanding the entity and its environment, including the entity's internal control, thereby providing a basis for designing and implementing responses to the assessed risks of material misstatement.'

In order to obtain this understanding of their clients the auditor must obtain information about the following matters:

- Relevant industry, regulatory and other external factors (including the financial reporting framework);
- The nature of the entity, including:
  - its operations;
  - its ownership and governance structures;
  - the types of investment it makes; and
  - the way it is structured and financed.
- The entity's selection and application of accounting policies;
- The entity's objectives, strategies and related business risks;
- The measurement and review of the entity's financial performance; and
- The internal controls relevant to the audit.

Once the auditor has obtained this information they must consider how the general business risks identified could impact the financial statements and if they could lead to material misstatement.

The information used to complete these references can come from a wide range of sources, including:

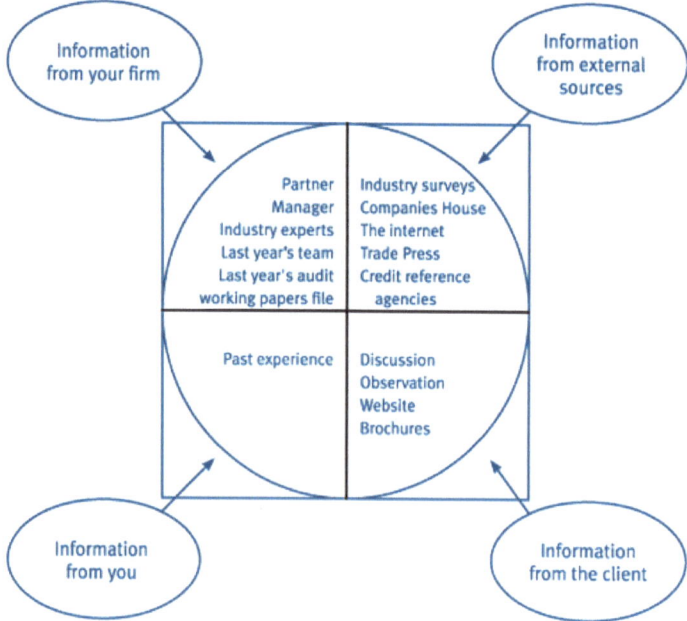

RISK ASSESSMENT PROCEDURES

ISA 315 requires auditors to perform the following procedures to understand the entity and its environment:

- Enquiries with management and others within the client entity (e.g. about external and internal changes the company has experienced);
- Analytical procedures; and
- Observation (e.g. of control procedures) and inspection (e.g. of key strategic documents and procedural manuals).

AUDITORS' RESPONSIBILITIES REGARDING FRAUD

Major scandals that have affected the accounting profession in recent times have usually been as a result of fraud. Therefore, in order to maintain confidence in the profession it is important for auditors and directors to understand their role in the prevention and detection of fraud.

ISA 240 the Auditor's Responsibilities Relating to Fraud in an Audit of Financial Statements recognises that misstatement in the financial statements can arise from either fraud or error. The distinguishing factor is whether the underlying action that resulted in the misstatement was intentional or unintentional.

It is important to note that fraud is a criminal activity. It is not the role of an auditor to determine whether fraud has actually occurred. That is the responsibility of a country's legal system. Auditors must be aware of the impact of both fraud and error on the accuracy of the financial statements.

Fraud can be further split into two types:

- Fraudulent financial reporting - deliberately misstating the accounts to make the company look better/worse than it actually is
- Misappropriation of assets - the theft of the company's assets such as cash or inventory.

The External Auditor's Responsibilities

The external auditor is responsible for obtaining reasonable assurance that the financial statements, taken as a whole, are free from material misstatement, whether caused by fraud or error. Therefore, the external auditor has some responsibility for considering the risk of material misstatement due to fraud.

In order to achieve this auditor must maintain an attitude of professional scepticism. This means that the auditor must recognise the possibility that a material misstatement due to fraud could occur, regardless of the auditor's prior experience of the client's integrity and honesty.

ISA 315 Identifying and Assessing the Risks of Material Misstatement Through Understanding the Entity and Its Environment goes further than this general concept and requires that engagement teams discuss the susceptibility of their clients to fraud. The engagement team should also obtain information for use in identifying the risk of fraud when performing risk assessment procedures.

To be able to make such an assessment auditors must identify, through enquiry, how management assesses and responds to the risk of fraud. The auditor must also enquire of management, internal auditors and those charged with governance if they are aware of any actual or suspected fraudulent activity.

Despite these requirements, owing to the inherent limitations of an audit, there is an unavoidable risk that some material misstatements may not be detected, even when the audit is planned and performed in accordance with ISAs. The risks in respect of fraud are higher than those for error because fraud may involve sophisticated and carefully organised schemes designed to conceal it.

Reporting Fraud

If the auditor identifies a fraud they should communicate the matter on a timely basis to the appropriate level of management (i.e. those with the primary responsibility for prevention and detection of fraud). If the suspected fraud involves management the auditor shall communicate such matters to those charged with governance. If the auditor has doubts about the integrity of those charged with governance they should seek legal advice regarding an appropriate course of action.

In addition to these responsibilities the auditor must also consider whether they have a responsibility to report the occurrence of a suspicion to a party outside the entity. Whilst the auditor does have an ethical duty to maintain confidentiality, it is likely that any legal responsibility will take precedent. In these circumstances it is advisable to seek legal advice.

Directors' Responsibilities

The directors have a primary responsibility for the prevention and detection of fraud. By implementing an effective system of internal control they should reduce the possibility of undetected fraud occurring to a minimum.

The directors should be aware of the potential for fraud and this should feature as an element of their risk assessment and corporate governance procedures. The audit committee should review these procedures to ensure that they are in place and working effectively. This will normally be done in conjunction with the internal auditors.

Internal auditors may be given an assignment:

- To assess the likelihood of fraud, or if a fraud has been discovered,
- To assess its consequences and
- To make recommendations for prevention in the future.

AUDIT PROCEDURES

As well as adopting an attitude of professional scepticism the auditor is required to perform the following procedures in light of the risk of fraud:

- Discussion amongst the engagement team regarding the susceptibility of the client to fraud;
- Consider the risk of fraud when documenting and testing internal controls;
- Enquiring of management how they: assess the risk of fraud; and identify and respond to the risks of fraud;
- Enquiring of management whether they have any knowledge of actual or suspected frauds;

- Enquiring of internal audit whether they have any knowledge of actual or suspected frauds;
- Enquiring of those charged with governance how they exercise oversight of management's process for identifying and responding to the risk of fraud; and
- Enquiring of those charged with governance whether they have any knowledge of actual or suspected frauds;

PROFESSIONAL SCEPTICISM

Definition
"An attitude that includes a questioning mind, being alert to conditions which may indicate possible misstatement due to fraud or error, and a critical assessment of audit evidence" (**ISA 200** Overall Objectives of the Independent Auditor and the Conduct of an Audit in Accordance with International Standards on Auditing)

Significance
Auditors are required to perform audits with an attitude of professional scepticism. There has been much criticism recently that auditors are failing in this requirement and there are plans to try and improve scepticism within the profession.

Practically auditors need to remain alert to the risk of misstatement, regardless of the perceived strength of the client's controls or the results of previous audit procedures (either in the current or prior years). A good example is fraud: no matter how strong a client's controls, fraud is always possible.

Another implication of scepticism is to consider the nature of identified misstatements. There has been a tendency in the past to immediately identify a misstatement as an error (i.e. accidental). Auditors should consider misstatements more deeply; they could be due to fraud, or at least indicative of deficiencies in the accounting system that could lead to further errors or frauds.

AUDIT RISK

Definition
Audit risk is the risk that the auditor expresses an inappropriate audit opinion.

The Risk Based Approach To Auditing
Modern auditing uses this approach, the main principle of which is explained in **ISA 200** Overall Objectives of the Independent Auditor and the Conduct of an Audit in Accordance with ISA's:

'To obtain reasonable assurance, the auditor shall obtain sufficient appropriate evidence to reduce audit risk to an acceptably low level.....'

This is further developed by **ISA 315** Identifying and Assessing the Risks of Material Misstatement Through Understanding the Entity and its Environment, which states:

'The objective of the auditor is to identify and assess the risk of material misstatement, whether due to fraud or error, at the financial statement and assertion levels, through understanding the entity and its environment, including the entity's internal control, thereby providing a basis for designing and implementing responses to the assessed risks of material misstatement.'

In simple terms:
- The auditor identifies the risk of material misstatement, and
- They use this to guide the design of their audit testing/procedures.

COMPONENTS OF AUDIT RISK

As stated previously; audit risk is the risk of that the auditor expresses an inappropriate audit opinion, i.e. that they give an unmodified audit opinion when the financial statements contain a material misstatement.

It can be further divided into the following sub-categories of risk:

Inherent risk

This is the susceptibility of a class of transaction, account balance or disclosure to a misstatement that could be material, either individually or in aggregate, before consideration of related controls. In other words this is the risk that a misstatement occurs in the first instance.

Inherent risk is often considered in relation to business risk. These are the risks resulting from conditions, events, circumstances, actions or inactions that could adversely affect an entity's ability to achieve its business objectives and goals. Ultimately these business risks can lead to complications and deficiencies in the accounting process, which could lead to fraud, error or omission.

Clearly this requires the audit team to have a good knowledge of how the client's activities are likely to affect its financial statements, and the audit team should discuss these matters in a planning meeting before deciding on the detailed approach and audit work to be used.

Control risk

This is the risk is that a misstatement will not be prevented, or detected and corrected on a timely basis by the entity's internal controls. This is either due to the internal control system being insufficient in the circumstances of the business or because the controls have not been applied effectively during the period.

We will consider internal control in depth later in the text.

Detection risk

This is the risk that the procedures performed by the auditor to reduce audit risk to an acceptable level will not detect potentially material misstatements, either individually or in aggregate. Detection risk comprises **sampling risk** and **non-sampling risk.**

Sampling risk is the risk that the auditor's conclusion based on a sample is different from the conclusion that would be reached if the whole population were tested (see sampling in the audit evidence chapter).

Non-sampling risk is the risk that the auditor's conclusion is inappropriate for any other reason, e.g. the application of inappropriate procedures or the failure to recognise a misstatement.

AUDITORS' RESPONSIBILITIES REGARDING LAWS AND REGULATIONS
Responsibilities of Management
Management are responsible for ensuring the entity they are responsible for complies with relevant laws and regulations, including:
- Company law, e.g. the UK Companies Act 2006;
- Corporate Governance law, e.g. the US Sarbanes Oxley Act 2002;
- Health and safety law;
- Employment law;
- Stock exchange rules; and
- Financial reporting regulations.

This requires the monitoring of legal requirements, the development of systems of internal control to ensure compliance and an effective system of assessing the effectiveness of those control systems.

Responsibilities of the Auditor
The auditor is responsible for obtaining reasonable assurance that the financial statements taken as a whole, are free from material misstatement, whether caused by fraud or error (ISA 200).

Non-compliance with laws and regulations can impact the financial statements because companies in breach of the law may need to make provisions for future legal costs and fines. In the worst case scenario this could affect the ability of the company to continue as a going concern.

In addition the auditor may need to report identified non-compliance with laws and regulations either to management or to a regulatory body, if the issue requires such action. An example of the latter would be when the client is in breach of money laundering regulations. Therefore, in planning an audit of financial statements the auditor must take into account the applicable legal and regulatory framework.

More specifically the auditor must obtain sufficient, appropriate evidence regarding compliance with those laws and regulations generally recognised to have a direct effect on the determination of material amounts and disclosures in the financial statements.

The auditor must also perform specified audit procedures to help identify instances of non-compliance with those laws and regulations that may have a material impact on the financial statements. If non-compliance is identified (or suspected) the auditor must then respond appropriately.

Audit Procedures
ISA 250 Consideration of Laws and Regulations in an Audit of Financial Statements requires an auditor to perform the following procedures:
- Obtaining a general understanding of the client's legal and regulatory environment;
- inspecting correspondence with relevant licensing and regulatory authorities;
- Enquiring of management and those charged with governance as to whether the entity is compliant with laws and regulations;
- Remaining alert to possible instances of non-compliance; and

- Obtaining written representations that the directors have disclosed all instances of known and possible non-compliance to the auditor.

CHAPTER FIVE
AUDIT EVIDENCE

ISA 330 The Auditor's Responses to Assessed Risks requires the auditor to design and perform audit procedures whose "nature, timing and extent are based on and are responsive to the assessed risks of material misstatement."

In essence the auditor has to obtain audit evidence sufficient to enable them to offer reasonable assurance that the financial statements are free from material misstatement. Therefore the selection and application of the procedures designed to achieve this are of vital importance to an effective audit.

Auditors are required to obtain sufficient and appropriate evidence to form an audit opinion. Modern auditing also requires consideration of a number of additional factors that affect the design of audit procedures, namely:

- The use of computer assisted audit techniques,
- The use of auditors' experts,
- The use of internal auditors, and
- The difficulties of auditing estimates.

Accounting Estimates
Examples

Common accounting estimates include:

- Inventory valuations (net realisable value; need for impairments)
- Depreciation method and useful life
- All provisions and contingent liabilities
- Irrecoverable debts and allowances for receivables
- Tangible asset valuations where revaluations have occurred

The problem with estimates

Accounting estimates are of particular concern to the auditor as, by their nature, there may not be any physical evidence to support them and they are prone to inaccuracy. They are also subjective and therefore prone to management bias. If the directors wished to manipulate the accounts in any way, accounting estimates are an easy way for them to do this. The auditor must take care when auditing estimates to ensure this has not been the case.

Procedures for auditing estimates

In accordance with **ISA 540** Auditing Accounting Estimates auditors need to obtain an understanding of:

- How management identifies those transactions, events and conditions that give rise to the need for estimates; and
- How management actually makes the estimates, including the control procedures in place to minimise the risk of misstatement.

ISA 540 also requires the auditor to:

- Evaluate the degree of uncertainty associated with an accounting estimate; and
- Consider if estimates with a high degree of uncertainty give rise to significant risks.

In response to this assessment auditors should perform the following further procedures:
- Review of the outcome of the estimates made in the prior period (or their subsequent re-estimation);
- Consider events after the reporting date that provide additional evidence about estimates made at the year-end;
- Test the basis and data upon which management made the estimate (e.g. review mathematical methods);
- Test the operating effectiveness of controls over how estimates are made;
- Develop an independent estimate to use as a point of comparison; and
- Consider whether specialist skills/knowledge are required (e.g. lawyer).

COMPUTER ASSISTED AUDIT TECHNIQUES (CAATS)

There are two broad categories of CAAT:
1. Audit software; and
2. Test data.

Audit software

Audit software is used to interrogate a client's system. It can be either packaged, off-the-shelf software or it can be purpose written to work on a client's system. The main advantage of these programs is that they can be used to scrutinise large volumes of data, which it would be inefficient to do manually. The programs can then present the results so that they can be investigated further.

Specific procedures they can perform include:
- Extracting samples according to specified criteria, such as:
  - Random;
  - Over a certain amount;
  - Below a certain amount;
  - At certain dates.
- Calculating ratios and select indicators that fail to meet certain pre-defined criteria (i.e. benchmarking);
- Check arithmetical accuracy (for example additions);
- Preparing reports (budget vs actual);
- Stratification of data (such as invoices by customer or age);
- Produce letters to send out to customers and suppliers; and
- Tracing transactions through the computerised system.

These procedures can simplify the auditor's task by selecting samples for testing, identifying risk areas and by performing certain substantive procedures. The software does not, however, replace the need for the auditor's own procedures.

Test data

Test data involves the auditor submitting 'dummy' data into the client's system to ensure that the system correctly processes it and that it prevents or detects and corrects misstatements. The objective of this is to test the operation of application controls within the system.

To be successful test data should include both data with errors built into it and data without errors. Examples of errors include:
- Codes that do not exist, e.g. customer, supplier and employee;
- Transactions above pre-determined limits, e.g. salaries above contracted amounts, credit above limits agreed with customer;
- Invoices with arithmetical errors; and
- Submitting data with incorrect batch control totals.

Data may be processed during a normal operational cycle ('live' test data) or during a special run at a point in time outside the normal operational cycle ('dead' test data). Both has their advantages and disadvantages:
- Live tests could interfere with the operation of the system or corrupt master files/standing data;
- Dead testing avoids this scenario but only gives assurance that the system works when not operating live. This may not be reflective of the strains the system is put under in normal conditions.

Advantages of CAATs
CAATs allow the auditor to:
- Independently access the data stored on a computer system without dependence on the client;
- Test the reliability of client software, i.e. the IT application controls (the results of which can then be used to assess control risk and design further audit procedures);
- Increase the accuracy of audit tests; and
- Perform audit tests more efficiently, which in the long-term will result in a more cost effective audit.

Disadvantages of CAATs
- CAATs can be expensive and time consuming to set up, the software must either be purchased or designed (in which case specialist IT staff will be needed);
- Client permission and cooperation may be difficult to obtain;
- Potential incompatibility with the client's computer system;
- The audit team may not have sufficient IT skills and knowledge to create the complex data extracts and programming required;
- The audit team may not have the knowledge or training needed to understand the results of the CAATs; and
- Data may be corrupted or lost during the application of CAATs.

OtherTtechniques
There are other forms of CAAT that are becoming increasingly common as computer technology develops, although the cost and sophistication involved currently limits their use to the larger accountancy firms with greater resources. These include:
Integrated test facilities - this involves the creation of dummy ledgers and records to which test data can be sent. This enables more frequent and efficient test data procedures to be

performed live and the information can simply be ignored by the client when printing out their internal records; and

Embedded audit software - this requires a purpose written audit program to be embedded into the client's accounting system. The program will be designed to perform certain tasks (similar to audit software) with the advantage that it can be turned on and off at the auditor's wish throughout the accounting year. This will allow the auditor to gather information on certain transactions (perhaps material ones) for later testing and will also identify peculiarities that require attention during the final audit.

USING THE WORK OF AN AUDITOR'S EXPERT
Why rely on the work of other people?
In certain circumstances auditors may need to rely on the work of, or consult parties not involved in the audit process. Auditors may also choose to rely on the work of others because they find it effective and efficient to do so.

Auditors do not need to be experts in all aspects of their clients' businesses. Where they lack the technical knowledge and skills to gather evidence about transactions, balances and disclosures they should seek the assistance of an expert. For example:

- Property valuation;
- Construction work in progress.
- Assessment of oil reserves;
- Specialist inventory - livestock, food and drink in the restaurant trade, jewelery; oil reserves; and
- Actuarial valuations for pension schemes.

Procedures involved in using and expert
ISA 620 Using the Work of an Auditor's Expert states that the auditor should obtain sufficient and appropriate evidence that the work of the expert is adequate for the purpose of the audit.

In making this assessment the external auditor must assess the expert's:
- Independence and objectivity; and
- Competence (i.e. qualifications, memberships of professional bodies and experience)

Before any work is performed by the expert the auditor should agree in writing:
- The nature, scope and objectives of the expert's work;
- The roles and responsibilities of the auditor and the expert;
- The nature, timing and extent of communication between the two parties; and
- The need for the expert to observe confidentiality.

Once the work has been completed the auditor must then assess it to ensure it is appropriate for the purposes of the audit. This involves consideration of:
- The consistency of the findings with other evidence;
- The significant assumptions made; and
- The use and accuracy of source data.

USING THE WORK OF INTERNAL AUDITORS

An internal audit department forms part of the client's system of internal control. If this is an effective element of the control system it may well reduce control risk, and therefore reduce the need for the auditor to perform detailed substantive testing. This will obviously be taken into account during the planning phase of the audit.

Additionally, auditors may be able to co-operate with a client's internal audit department and place reliance on their procedures in place of performing their own.

Procedures for using Internal Audit

ISA 610 Using the Work of Internal Auditors states that before relying on the work of internal auditors, the external auditor must determine whether it is likely to be adequate for the purposes of the audit. This involves an evaluation of:

- The objectivity of the internal audit function;
- The technical competence of the internal audit function;
- Whether the internal audit function is carried out with due professional care; and
- Whether there is likely to be effective communication between the internal and external auditor.

If the auditor considers it appropriate to use the work of the internal audit function they then have to incorporate this into their planning to assess the impact on the nature, timing and extent of further audit procedures. They also have to plan adequate time to review the work of the internal audit function to evaluate whether:

- The work was performed by people with adequate technical training and proficiency;
- The work was properly supervised, reviewed and documented;
- Sufficient and appropriate evidence has been obtained to be able to draw reasonable conclusions;
- The conclusions reached are appropriate in the circumstances; and
- Any unusual matters are properly resolved.

Sufficient, Appropriate Evidence

"The objective of the auditor is to design and perform audit procedures in such a way to enable the auditor to **obtain sufficient appropriate audit evidence to be able to draw reasonable conclusions** on which to base the auditor's opinion.' (**ISA 500** Audit Evidence)

- Sufficiency relates to the quantity of evidence.
- Appropriateness relates to the quality and reliability of evidence.

Sufficient evidence

There needs to be 'enough' evidence to support the auditor's conclusion. What is 'enough' at the end of the day is a matter of professional judgement. However, when determining whether they have enough evidence on file the auditor must consider:

- The risk of material misstatement;
- The materiality of the item;
- The nature of accounting and internal control systems;
- The auditor's knowledge and experience of the business;
- The results of controls tests;

- The size of a population being tested;
- The size of the sample selected to test; and
- The reliability of the evidence obtained.

Consider, for example, the audit of a bank balance:

Auditors will confirm year-end bank balances directly with the bank. This is a good source of evidence but on its own is not sufficient to give assurance regarding the completeness and final valuation of bank and cash amounts. The key reason is timing differences. The client may have received cash amounts or cheques before the end of the year, or may have paid out cheques before the end of the year, that have not yet cleared the bank account. For this reason the auditor should also perform a bank reconciliation.

In combination these two pieces of evidence will be sufficient to give assurance over the bank balances.

Appropriate evidence

Appropriateness of evidence breaks down into two important concepts:

- Reliability; and
- Relevance.

Reliability

Auditors should always attempt to obtain evidence from the most trustworthy and dependable source possible. Evidence is considered more reliable when it is:

- Obtained from an independent external source;
- Generated internally but subject to effective control;
- Obtained directly by the auditor;
- In documentary form; and
- In original form.

Broadly speaking, the more reliable the evidence the less of it the auditor will need. However the converse is not necessarily true: if evidence is unreliable it will never be appropriate for the audit, no matter how much is gathered.

Relevance

To be relevant audit evidence has to address the objective/purpose of a procedure. For example:

Attendance at an inventory count provides us with a good example of the relevance of procedures. During counting the auditor considers the relationship between inventory records and physical inventories, as follows:

- Identifying items of physical inventory and tracing them to inventory records to confirm the **completeness** of accounting records; and
- Identifying items on the inventory record and tracing them to physical inventories to confirm the **existence** of inventory assets.

Whilst the procedures are perhaps similar in nature their purpose (and relevance) is to test different assertions regarding inventory balances.

CHAPTER SIX
AUDIT COMPLETION

Although it sounds as though this takes place at the end of the audit, after the obtaining of audit evidence, this is not necessarily the case. Completion simply refers to all those necessary tasks that must be completed before the audit opinion can be decided and the audit procedures concluded. Many of the tasks listed below are on-going; starting during the planning phase and continuing on until after the audit report has been signed.

The tasks include consideration of:

- Opening Balances,
- Comparative Information,
- Subsequent Events, and
- Going Concern.

In addition, there are certain tasks that naturally occur towards the end of the audit process, once all other procedures have been completed. These include:

- Obtaining written representations,
- The final review of the audit file, and
- Evaluating identified misstatements.

AUDITING OPENING BALANCES

Introduction

ISA 510 Initial Engagements - Opening Balances requires that when auditors take on a new client, they must ensure that:

- Opening balances do not contain material misstatements;
- Prior period closing balances have been correctly brought forward or, where appropriate, restated; and
- Appropriate accounting policies have been consistently applied, or changes adequately disclosed.

Considerations

- Were the previous financial statements audited?
- If the previous financial statements were audited, was the opinion modified?
- If the previous opinion was modified, has the matter been resolved since then?
- Were any adjustments made as a result of the audit? If so, has the client adjusted their accounting ledgers as well as the financial statements?

If auditors are unable to satisfy themselves with regard to the preceding period, they will have to consider modifying the current audit report.

Procedures

Where the prior period was audited by another auditor or unaudited, the auditors will need to perform additional work in order to satisfy themselves regarding the opening position. Such work would include:

- Consulting the client's management
- Reviewing records and accounting and control procedures in the preceding period

- Consulting with the previous auditor and reviewing (with their permission) their working papers and relevant management letters
- Substantive testing of any opening balances where the above procedures are unsatisfactory.

Some evidence of the opening position will also usually be gained from the audit work performed in the current period.

COMPARATIVE INFORMATION

Introduction

ISA 710 Comparative Information - Corresponding Figures and Comparative Financial Statements requires that comparative figures comply with the identified financial reporting framework and that they are free from material misstatement.

The IASB's Framework for the Preparation and Presentation of Financial Statements and IAS 1 Presentation of Financial Statements both require that financial statements show comparatives.

Categories of Comparative

- Corresponding figures where preceding period figures are included as an integral part of the current period financial statements; and
- Comparative financial statements where preceding period amounts are included for comparison with the current period.

Corresponding Figures

Audit procedures in respect of corresponding figures should be significantly less than for the current period and are limited to ensuring that corresponding figures have been correctly reported and appropriately classified. This involves evaluating whether:

- Accounting policies are consistently applied; and
- Corresponding figures agree to the prior period financial statements.

Comparative financial statements

Sufficient appropriate evidence should be gathered to ensure that comparative financial statements meet the requirements of an applicable financial reporting framework. This involves evaluating whether:

- accounting policies are consistently applied; and
- comparative figures agree to the prior period financial statements.

EVALUATION OF MISSTATEMENTS

Communication

In accordance with **ISA 450** Evaluation of Misstatements Identified During the Audit all misstatements should be communicated to management on a timely basis, unless they are clearly trivial. Management should be asked to correct all misstatements identified during the audit. Auditors should try and obtain an understanding of management's reasons for refusing to adjust any of the misstatements. The auditor should determine whether uncorrected misstatements are material in aggregate or individually, and if material should consider the potential impact on their audit report.

Materiality
Prior to evaluating the significance of uncorrected misstatements the auditor should reassess materiality to confirm whether it remains appropriate to the financial statements. Then the auditor must assess whether uncorrected misstatements are, individually or in aggregate, material. To do this they should consider the size and nature of the misstatements, both in relation to the financial statements as a whole and to particular classes of transaction, account balances and disclosures.

WRITTEN REPRESENTATIONS
Finally, the auditor should obtain a written representation from management and those charged with governance that they believe the effect of the uncorrected misstatements is immaterial, individually and in aggregate.
Once these procedures have been completed the auditor should then consider the impact of uncorrected misstatements on the audit report.

GOING CONCERN
Definition
According to IAS1 financial statements should be prepared on the basis that the company is a going concern unless it is inappropriate to do so.
It is defined in IAS1 as the assumption that the enterprise will continue in operational existence for the foreseeable future.

Challenges assessing going concern
- Any consideration involving the 'foreseeable future' involves making a judgement about future events, which are inherently uncertain.
- Uncertainty increases with time and judgements can only be made on the basis of information available at any point - subsequent events can overturn that judgement.
- The period that management (and therefore the auditor) is required to consider is usually defined by financial reporting standards. Generally (but not exclusively) the period is a minimum of twelve months from the year-end, with twelve months from the date the financial statements are published being preferred.
- There may be circumstances in which it is appropriate to look further ahead. This depends on the nature of the business and their associated risks.

Significance for the financial statements
Whether or not a company can be classed as a going concern affects how its financial statements are prepared.
- Financial statements are usually prepared on the basis that the reporting entity is a going concern.
- IAS1 states that 'an entity should prepare its financial statements on a going concern basis, unless

- o The entity is being liquidated or has ceased trading, or
- o The directors have no realistic alternative but to liquidate the entity or to cease trading.'
- Where the assumption is made that the company will cease trading, the financial statements are prepared using the **break-up basis** under which:
  - o Assets are recorded at likely sale values
  - o Inventory and receivables are likely to require more provisions, and
  - o Additional liabilities may arise (severance costs for staff, the costs of closing down facilities, etc.).

Directors' Responsibilities
- It is the directors' responsibility to assess the company's ability to continue as a going concern when they are preparing the financial statements.
- If they are aware of any material uncertainties which may affect this assessment, then IAS 1 requires them to disclose such uncertainties in the financial statements.
- When the directors are performing their assessment they should take into account a number of relevant factors such as:
  - o Current and expected profitability
  - o Debt repayment
  - o Sources (and potential sources) of financing.

Auditors' Responsibilities
- **ISA 570** Going Concern states that the auditor needs to consider the appropriateness of management's use of the going concern assumption.
- The auditors need to assess the risk that the company may not be a going concern.
- The auditor will also need to obtain sufficient appropriate evidence that the company is a going concern.
- Where there are going concern issues, the auditor needs to ensure that the directors have made sufficient disclosure of such matters in the notes to the financial statements.

Procedures

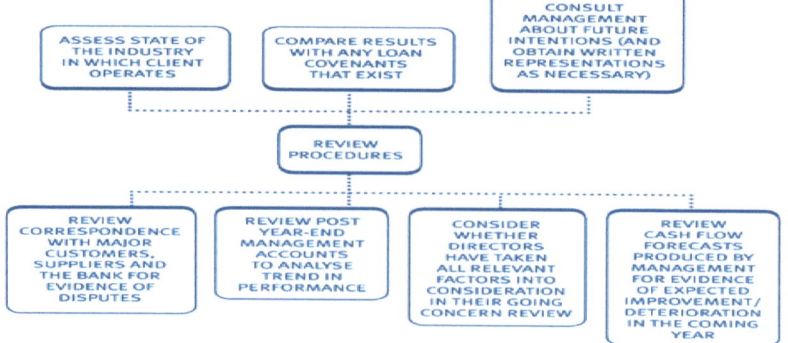

Indicators of Going Concern Problems

Typical indicators and explanations of going concern problems include the following:

- Net current liabilities (or net liabilities overall!); indicates an inability to meet debts as they fall due.
- Borrowing facilities not agreed or close to expiry of current agreement; lack of access to cash may make it difficult for a company to manage its operating cycle.
- Defaulted loan agreements; loans normally become repayable on default, company may find it difficult to repay loan.
- Unplanned sales of non-current assets; indicates an inability to generate cash from other means and as non-current assets generate income, will cause a decline in income and therefore profits.
- Missing tax payments; results in fines and penalties, companies normally prioritise tax payments indicating a lack of working capital.
- Failure to pay staff; indicates a significant lack of working capital.
- Negative cash flow; indicates overtrading.
- Inability to obtain credit from suppliers; suggests failure to pay suppliers on time and working capital problems.
- Major technology changes; inability or insufficient funds to keep up with changes in technology will result in loss of custom and obsolescence of inventory.
- Legal claims; successful legal claims may result in significant cash payments that can only be settled with liquidation.
- Loss of key staff; may result inability to trade.
- Over-reliance on a small number of products, staff , suppliers or customers; loss may result in inability to trade.

Disclosures

Where there is any significant doubt over the future of a company, the directors should include disclosures in the financial statements explaining:

- the nature of and circumstances surrounding the doubts; and
- the possible effect on the company.

Where the directors have been unable to assess going concern in the usual way (e.g. for less than one year beyond the date on which they sign the financial statements), this fact should be disclosed.

Where the financial statements are prepared on a basis other than the going concern basis, the basis used should be disclosed.

SUBSEQUENT EVENTS

Managements' Responsibilities

Management are responsible for preparing the financial statements in accordance with the relevant financial reporting framework. IAS 10 Events After the Reporting Period requires management to consider the impact of events that occur after the year-end on the financial statements. It categorises those events as either:

- Adjusting events, which provide evidence of conditions that existed at the year-end, and therefore should be considered in the transactions, balances and disclosures of the financial statements, and

- Non-adjusting events, which concern conditions that arose after the year-end and are therefore relevant to the following period's financial statements. If serious though (i.e. they could have a material impact on the business) these may need to be disclosed in the financial statements.

THE AUDITORS' RESPONSIBILITIES

ISA 560 Subsequent Events details the responsibilities of the auditors with respect to subsequent events and the procedures they can use. It identifies two periods of relevance:

Up to the date of the audit report

Until this point the auditor must perform procedures to identify events that need to be either adjusted or disclosed in the financial statements.

Between the date of the audit report and publishing the accounts

During this period the auditor need not perform procedures but, if they identify any adjustments or disclosures that need to be made in the financial statements they must take appropriate action.

This will normally be in the form of requesting that the directors amend the financial statements and then reissuing the audit report.

If the directors refuse then the auditor has the right to communicate the known misstatements to the shareholders at the annual general meeting. The auditor may also consider resigning and issuing a statement of circumstance.

Procedures

The nature of procedures performed in a subsequent events review depends on many variables, such as the nature of transactions and events and the availability of data and reports. However the following procedures are typical of a subsequent events review:

- Enquiring into management's procedures/systems for the identification of subsequent events;
- Inspection of minutes of members' and directors' meetings;
- Reviewing accounting records including budgets, forecasts and interim information.
- Enquiring of directors if they are aware of any subsequent events that require reflection in the year-end account;
- Obtaining, from management, a letter of representation that all subsequent events have been considered in the preparation of the financial statements;
- Inspection of correspondence with legal advisors;
- Enquiring of the progress with regards to reported provisions and contingencies; and
- 'Normal' post reporting period work performed in order to verify year-end balances:
  - checking after date receipts from receivables;
  - inspecting the cash book for payments/receipts that were not accrued for at the year-end; and
  - checking the sales price of inventories.

If, after the financial statements have been issued, management amends the financial statements, the auditor shall:

- Provide a new auditor's report on the amended financial statements; and
- Extend the audit procedures described above to the date of the new auditor's report.

WRITTEN REPRESENTATIONS

Definition
A written representation is a (written) statement by management provided to the auditor to confirm certain matters or to support other audit evidence (**ISA 580** Written Representations).

Purpose
The purpose of obtaining this form of evidence is twofold:
- To obtain representations that management, and those charged with governance, have fulfilled their responsibility for the preparation of the financial statements, including;
  - Preparing the financial statements in accordance with an applicable financial reporting framework;
  - Providing the auditor with all relevant information and access to records;
  - Recording all transactions and reflecting them in the financial statements.
- To support other audit evidence relevant to the financial statements if determined necessary by the auditor or required by ISA's.

The latter point may be relevant where the auditor deems that other, more reliable forms of evidence are not available to them. Examples include:
- Plans or intentions that may affect the carrying value of assets or liabilities;
- Confirmation of values where there is a significant degree of estimation or judgement involved, e.g. provisions and contingent liabilities;
- Formal confirmation of the directors' judgement on contentious issues, e.g. the value of assets where there is a risk of impairment; and
- Aspects of laws and regulations that may affect the financial statements, including compliance.

How are Written Representations Obtained?
As the audit progresses, the audit team will assemble a list of those items about which it is appropriate to seek management representations. During completion the auditors will write to the client confirming the issues about which they are seeking representations. The clients must formally document, and sign, a response and send it to the auditor.

The representations themselves may take any of the following forms:
- A letter from the client to the auditors responding to the necessary points. (It is common for the auditor to draft the letter for the client, who simply reproduces it on their own letter-headed paper, approves it and signs it).
- A letter from the auditors to management setting out the necessary points, which management signs in acknowledgement and returns to the auditors.
- Minutes of a meeting where representations were made orally, which can be signed by management.

QUALITY AND RELIABILITY

Unfortunately, written representations are internal sources of evidence, and are therefore subject to bias, and tend to focus on contentious areas of the financial statements. They are therefore potentially unreliable forms of audit evidence. **ISA 580** also clearly states that written representations should only be sought to support other audit evidence. They do not, on their own, constitute sufficient evidence.

It is clear that the quality of written representations is somewhat dubious. However, there are instances where no other, better quality forms of evidence are available to the auditor, particularly where disclosures in the financial statements are restricted to matters of management judgement. Before they can be used the auditor must consider their reliability in terms of:

- Inconsistencies with other forms of evidence; and
- Concerns about the competence, integrity, ethical values or diligence of management;

With inconsistency the auditor will be required to reconsider their initial risk assessment and, perhaps, perform further procedures. If the latter is true (about competence, integrity etc) then the audit must consider whether the engagement can be conducted effectively. If they conclude that it cannot then they should withdraw, where permitted by laws and regulations. If they are not permitted to withdraw they should consider the impact on the audit report. It is likely that this would lead to them disclaiming their opinion.

The last point is also relevant if management refuses to provide written representations.

Additional Matters Requiring Written Representation

In addition to the matters identified in the passages above, the following issues may also be documented in a written representation:

- Directors have assessed the risk of fraud and consider it to be low;
- Directors are not aware of any actual, or suspected, instances of fraud;
- All related parties have been identified and transactions with them disclosed in the financial statements;
- Directors consider the aggregate of all uncorrected misstatements to be immaterial;
- The directors have considered all subsequent events in preparing the financial statements; and
- The directors have considered all possible events, matters and contingencies in performing their going concern review.

CHAPTER SEVEN
THE AUDIT REPORT

Objectives

The objectives of an auditor, in accordance with **ISA 700** Forming an Opinion and Reporting on Financial Statements are:

- To form an opinion on the financial statements based upon an evaluation of their conclusions drawn from audit evidence; and
- To express clearly that opinion through a written report.

Forming an opinion

The auditor forms an opinion on whether the financial statements are prepared, in all material respects, in accordance with the applicable financial reporting framework. In order to do that they must conclude whether they have obtained reasonable assurance about whether the financial statements as a whole are free from material misstatement (whether due to fraud or error)

In particular the auditor should evaluate whether:

- The financial statements adequately disclose the significant accounting policies;
- The accounting policies selected are consistently applied and appropriate;
- Accounting estimates are reasonable;
- Information is relevant, reliable, comparable and understandable;
- The financial statements provide adequate disclosures to enable the users to understand the effects of material transactions and events; and
- The terminology used is appropriate.

Auditor's conclusions

Unmodified reports

When the auditor concludes that the financial statements are prepared, in all material respects, in accordance with the applicable financial reporting framework and there are no additional matters to report they issue an unmodified.

Modified reports

If, however, the auditor concludes that either:

- The financial statements as a whole are not free from material misstatement,
- They have been unable to obtain sufficient appropriate evidence, or
- There are additional matters to report, then they have to issue a modified audit report

MODIFIED AUDIT REPORTS

Types of audit report

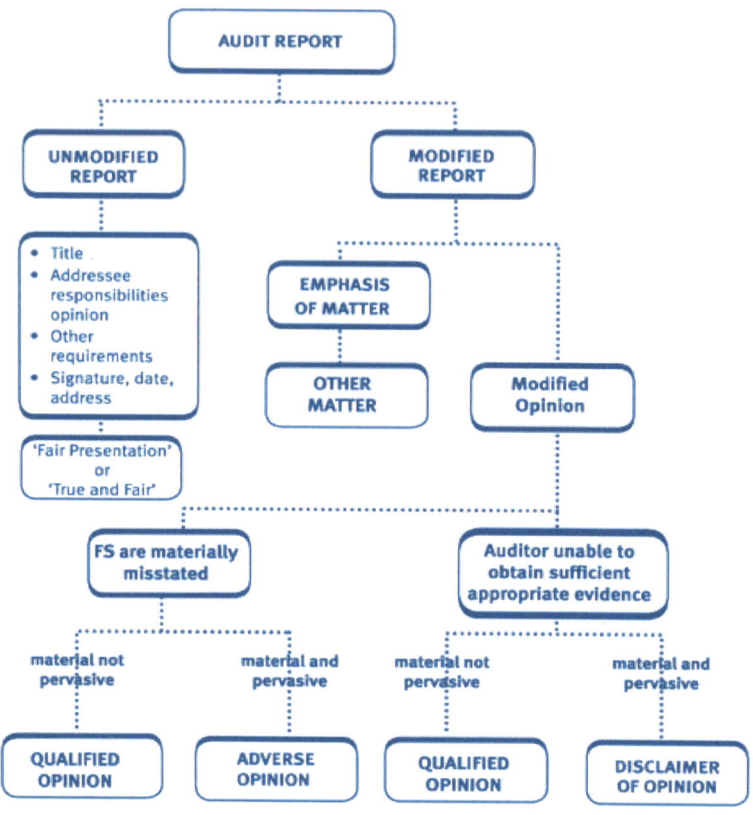

When the auditor concludes that the financial statements are prepared, in all material respects, in accordance with the applicable financial reporting framework and there are no additional matters to report they issue an unmodified audit report.

Types of modification

If, however, the auditor concludes that either:

- The financial statements as a whole are not free from material misstatement,
- They have been unable to obtain sufficient appropriate evidence, or
- There are additional matters to report,

Then they have to issue a modified audit report. There are two ways the audit report may be modified:

- By modifying the audit opinion, or
- Through inclusion of additional paragraphs in the audit report.

MODIFIED AUDIT OPINIONS

Reasons for modifying the opinion

There are two reasons why an auditor would be unable to give an unmodified audit opinion:

- They conclude that the financial statements as a whole are not free from material misstatements; or
- They have been unable to obtain sufficient appropriate evidence to conclude that the financial statements as a whole are free from material misstatement.

Materiality and Pervasiveness

If the auditor comes to either of the above conclusions they must then consider how significant the matter is. If the matter is considered immaterial then it should not affect the wording of the opinion and a 'present fairly' or 'true and fair' wording may be used. However, if the auditor concludes that the matter is material they must modify the wording of their opinion. If, in addition to being material, the auditor considers the matter to be pervasive to the financial statements, then this must also be incorporated into the audit opinion (as shown below). Pervasive means that the matter is:

- Not confined to specific elements of the financial statements;
- If confined represents a substantial proportion of the financial statements; or
- Is fundamental to users understanding of the financial statements.

Wording a modified opinion

The effects on the wording of the opinion can be summarised as follows:

	Auditor's Judgement Regarding the Pervasiveness of the Matter	
Nature of Matter	Material but Not Pervasive	Material and Pervasive
Financial statements are materially misstated	Qualified opinion	Adverse opinion
Inability to obtain sufficient appropriate evidence	Qualified opinion	Disclaimer of opinion

When the auditor modifies their opinion they have to include a 'Basis for Modification Paragraph' in the audit report that describes the matter giving rise to the modification. This paragraph should be placed before the opinion paragraph.

With a qualified opinion the auditor is basically stating that whilst there are, or maybe, material misstatements, they are confined to a specific element of the financial statements but the remainder may be relied upon. Accordingly the opinion usually states that "except for the matters described in the basis for modification paragraph, the financial statements present fairly (or give a true and fair view of) ...."

If the auditor concludes that the matter is pervasive they are claiming that the financial statements may not be relied upon in any part. Accordingly:

- If they give an adverse opinion they will state that the financial statements "do not present fairly (or give a true and fair view of)........."
- If they give a disclaimer they will state that they "do not express an opinion on the financial statements."

Illustration of a qualified opinion

Example of wording where the auditor concludes that the financial statements contain a material, but not pervasive, misstatement:

Basis for Qualified Opinion

As discussed in Note X to the financial statements, no depreciation has been provided in the financial statements which practice, in our opinion, is not in accordance with International Financial Reporting Standards. The provision for the year ended 31 December, 20X9, should be $xxx based on the straight-line method of depreciation using annual rates of 5% for the building and 20% for the equipment. Accordingly, the non-current assets should be reduced by accumulated depreciation of $xxx and the loss for the year and accumulated deficit should be increased by $xxx and $xxx, respectively.

Opinion

In our opinion, except for the effect on the financial statements of the matter referred to in the Basis for Qualified Opinion paragraph, the financial statements present fairly in all material respects (or give a true and fair view of) the financial position ....(remainder of wording as per an unmodified report).

Illustration of a qualified opinion

Example where the auditor concludes that they have been unable to gather sufficient appropriate evidence and the possible effects are deemed to be material but not pervasive

Basis for Qualified Opinion

We did not observe the counting of the physical inventories as at 31 December 20X9, since that date was prior to our appointment as auditor to the company. Owing to the nature of the company's records, we were unable to satisfy ourselves as to inventory quantities by other audit procedures.

Qualified Opinion

In our opinion, except for the possible effects of the matter described in the Basis for Qualified Opinion paragraph, the financial statements present fairly (or give a true and fair view of) the financial position............

Illustration of an adverse opinion

Example where the auditor concludes that the financial statements are materially and pervasively misstated:

Basis for Adverse Opinion
As explained in Note X, the company has recognised a number of assets acquired under a lease and the associated liabilities at a fair value of $xxx, accounting for the leases as a finance leases. The fair value of these assets represent 80% of total assets. Under International Financial Reporting Standards the leases should have been classified as operating leases. The companies records indicate that had the leases been correctly accounted for as operating leases....[explanation of the various effects on the amounts presented in the financial statements].

Adverse Opinion
In our opinion, because of the significance of the matter discussed in the Basis for Adverse Opinion paragraph , the financial statements do not present fairly (or give a true and fair view of) the financial position.......

Illustration of a disclaimer of opinion
Example where the auditor concludes that they have been unable to gather sufficient appropriate evidence and the possible effects are deemed to be both material and pervasive.

Basis for Disclaimer of Opinion
A new computerised payroll system was introduced in October 20X1, that has caused significant errors in the payroll records, amounts paid to employees, and taxation paid in the year. At the date of our audit report, management was still in the process of identifying and quantifying the volume and amount of errors, and rectifying and correcting the system and errors that have arisen. We were unable to confirm or verify by alternative means the payroll expense of $xxx, included in the income statement for the year ended 31 December 20X1, and associated liabilities of $xxx owed to the tax authorities and affected employees in the statement of financial position as at 31 December 20X1.
As a result, we were unable to determine whether any adjustments to the financial statements might have been necessary in respect of recorded or unrecorded liabilities or expenses, and the associated elements of the statement of changes in equity and cash flow statement.

Disclaimer of Opinion
Because of the significance of the matter described in the Basis of Disclaimer of Opinion paragraph, we have not been able to obtain sufficient appropriate evidence to provide a basis for an audit opinion. Accordingly, we do not express an opinion on the financial statements.

MODIFICATION THROUGH ADDITIONAL PARAGRAPHS
Types of additional paragraph
Having formed their opinion there are circumstances where the auditor must also draw the users attention to additional matters that are significant to their understanding of the financial statements. These circumstances are categorised as follows:
- Matters already presented/disclosed in the financial statements that are fundamental to understanding the financial statements. These are presented in "emphasis of matter" paragraphs; and

- Other matters relevant to understanding the audit, the auditor's responsibilities or the audit report. These are presented in "other matter" paragraphs.

Emphasis of matter paragraphs

These are presented immediately after the opinion paragraph. It is important to note that they have do not affect the audit opinion, nor are they a substitute for one.

These paragraphs simply draw the readers' attention to a note already disclosed in the financial statements. The matters referred to have to be fundamental to the readers' understanding of the financial statements. Widespread use of them would diminish their effectiveness.

Examples of where it may be necessary to add an emphasis of matter paragraph include:

- An uncertainty relating to the future outcome of exceptional litigation or regulatory action;
- Early application of a new accounting standards that has a pervasive effect on the financial statements;
- A major catastrophe that has had, or continues to have, a significant effect on the entity's financial position.

Other matter paragraphs

Circumstances where these may be necessary include:

- When a pervasive inability to obtain sufficient appropriate evidence is imposed by management (e.g. denying the auditor access to books and records) but the auditor is unable to withdraw from the engagement due to legal restrictions;
- When national laws/regulations require, or permit, the auditor to elaborate on their responsibilities;
- When the client issues another set of financial statements (e.g. one according to IFRS and one according to UK GAAP) and the auditor has also issued a report on those financial statements;
- When a set of financial statements is prepared for a specific purpose and user group and the users have determined that a general purpose framework meets their financial information needs; and
- If there is a material inconsistency between the audited financial statements and the 'other information' contained in the annual report (such as the Chairman's Report).

Illustration of an emphasis of matter paragraph

Emphasis of Matter

We draw attention to Note X to the financial statements. The Company is the defendant in a lawsuit alleging infringement of certain patent rights and claiming royalties and punitive damages. The Company has filed a counter action, and preliminary hearings and discovery proceedings on both actions are in progress. The ultimate outcome of the matter cannot presently be determined, and no provision for any liability that may result has been made in the financial statements. Our opinion is not qualified in respect of this matter.

UNMODIFIED AUDIT REPORTS

Introduction

ISA 700 Forming an Opinion and Reporting on Financial Statements provides guidance as to the nature and wording of the audit report. Most importantly the report must be in writing. In addition it recommends that the audit report be broken into distinct sections that explain the purpose, nature and scope of an audit. The main reason for this is to ensure that the users of the audit report understand the nature of audit procedures and that only reasonable assurance is being offered. One of the primary purposes of this is to reduce the 'expectations gap.'

The recommended elements of the report are as follows:

Title

- The title should be 'appropriate'. The use of 'Independent Auditor's Report' distinguishes this report from any other report produced internally or by other non-statutory auditors.

Addressee

- The report should be addressed to the intended user of the report which is usually the shareholders, or other parties as required by the circumstances of the engagement.

Introductory paragraph

- Identifies the entity whose financial statements have been audited;
- States that the financial statements have been audited;
- Identifies the components of the financial statements (by name and even page reference);
- Refers to the accounting policies applied to the financial statements; and
- Specifies the date or period covered by the financial statements.

Statement of responsibilities of management

- Preparation of the financial statements in accordance with the applicable financial reporting framework; and
- Designing and implementing an effective internal control system to enable the preparation of financial statements that are free of material misstatement;

Statement of responsibilities of the auditors

- Express an opinion.
- The audit was conducted in accordance with ISA's;
- Requirement to comply with ethical standards;
- The fact that the audit was planned and performed to obtain reasonable assurance about whether the financial statements are free from material misstatement.
- Audit involves procedures designed to obtain evidence about amounts and disclosures in the financial statements;
- The procedures are based upon auditor judgement, including a risk assessment and consideration of internal controls;
- Obtain sufficient, appropriate audit evidence on which to base the opinion.

Auditor's opinion (headed 'Opinion')

- When expressing an unmodified opinion the auditor (unless otherwise required by relevant laws or regulations) uses one of the following phrases:
  - "The financial statements present fairly, in all material respects........"; or
  - "The financial statements show a true and fair view of ....".

Auditor's signature

- The report may be signed in the name of the firm, or the personal name of the auditor, as appropriate for the particular jurisdiction.
- There may also be a requirement to state the auditor's professional accountancy designation or that the firm is recognised by the appropriate licensing authority (i.e. that the firm/partner is a member of a recognised supervisory body and is registered to audit).

Date of report

- The audit report should be dated no earlier that the date on which the auditor has obtained sufficient appropriate evidence upon which to base their opinion.
- This requires that all the statements and notes/disclosure that comprise the financial statements are finalised and that those with responsibility for preparation of the financial statements have acknowledged their role.
- Practically this means that the auditor should sign their report after the directors have approved the financial statements.

Auditor's address

- The audit report should name a specific location, which is normally the city where the auditor maintains the office that has responsibility for the audit.

Illustration

INDEPENDENT AUDITOR'S REPORT

(Appropriate Addressee)

Report on the Financial Statements

We have audited the accompanying financial statements of the ABC Company, which comprise the statement of financial position as at 31 December, 20X1, and the income statement, statement of changes in equity and cash flow statement for the year then ended, and a summary of significant accounting policies and other explanatory information.
Management's Responsibility for the Financial Statements
Management is responsible for the preparation and fair presentation of these financial statements in accordance with International Financial Reporting Standards, and for such internal control as management determines necessary to enable the preparation of financial statements that are free from material misstatement, whether due to fraud or error.

Auditor's Responsibility

Our responsibility is to express an opinion on these financial statements based on our audit. We conducted our audit in accordance with International Standards on Auditing. Those

Standards require that we comply with ethical requirements and plan and perform the audit to obtain reasonable assurance about whether the financial statements are free from material misstatement.

An audit involves performing procedures to obtain audit evidence about the amounts and disclosures in the financial statements. The procedures selected depend on the auditor's judgement, including the assessment of the risks of material misstatement of the financial statements, whether due to fraud or error. In making those risk assessments, the auditor considers internal control relevant to the entity's preparation and fair presentation of the financial statements in order to design audit procedures that are appropriate in the circumstances, but not for the purpose of expressing an opinion on the effectiveness of the entity's internal control. An audit also includes evaluating the appropriateness of accounting policies used and the reasonableness of accounting estimates made by management, as well as evaluating the presentation of the financial statements.

We believe that the audit evidence we have obtained is sufficient and appropriate to provide a basis for our audit opinion.

Opinion

In our opinion, the financial statements present fairly, in all material respects (or *give a true and fair view of*) the financial position of ABC Company as at December 31 20X1, and (*of*) its financial performance and its cash flows for the year then ended in accordance with International Financial Reporting Standards.

Auditor's signature

[Date of auditor's report]
[Auditor's address]
(**ISA 700,** appendix 1)

REPORTING TO THOSE CHARGED WITH GOVERNANCE

ISAs, in particular **ISA 260** Communication with Those Charged with Governance and **ISA 265** Communicating Deficiencies in Internal Control to Those Charged with Governance and Management, require the external auditors to engage in communications with management. The main forms of formal communication between the auditors and management are: the engagement letter; and another written communication, usually sent at the end of the audit, which is often referred to as 'the management letter.'

Objectives

The objectives of these communications are:
- To communicate the responsibilities of the auditor and an overview of the scope and timing of the audit;
- To obtain, from those charged with governance, information relevant to the audit;
- To provide timely observations arising from the audit that are significant to the responsibilities of those charged with governance; and
- To promote effective two-way communication between the auditor and those charged with governance.

Whilst a formal communication is usually sent at the conclusion of the audit there may be a need to communicate particular matters at other times to help meet the third objective, for example; if a fraud is discovered.

Matters to be communicated

Audit matters of governance interest include:

- Auditor independence;
- Effects of significant accounting policies and changes to them;
- Potential financial effect of risks/uncertainties;
- Material audit adjustments;
- Disagreements with management concerning the financial statements;
- Significant difficulties encountered during the audit;
- Expected modifications to the audit report; and
- Significant internal control deficiencies, including fraud.

Timing of communications

Stage of audit	Communication required
Planning	Practical matters concerning forthcoming audit.
	Independence of auditor.
	Expected fees.
	Nature and scope of audit work.
	Ensure letter of engagement is up to date.
During the audit	If any situation occurs and it would not be appropriate to delay communication until the audit is concluded.
Conclusion of audit	Major findings from audit work.
	Uncorrected misstatements.
	Qualitative aspects of accounting/reporting practices.
	Final draft of letter of representation.
	Expected modifications to audit report.
	Significant internal control deficiencies.

REFFERENCE

"Audit assurance".

McKenna, Francine. "Auditors and Audit Reports: Is The Firm's "John Hancock" Enough?". *Forbes*. Retrieved 22 July 2011.

"CONCEPT RELEASE ON POSSIBLE REVISIONS TO PCAOB STANDARDS RELATED TO REPORTS ON AUDITED FINANCIAL STATEMENTS". Retrieved 22 July 2011.

Pages - Definition of Internal Auditing". Na.theiia.org. 2000-01-01. Retrieved 2013-09-02.

"Pages - International Professional Practices Framework (IPPF)". Na.theiia.org. 2000-01-01. Retrieved 2013-09-02.

"Professional internal auditors, in carrying out their responsibilities, apply COSO's Integrated Framework-Internal Control". Theiia.org.

Different Types of Audits (June 2013) Auditronix Guidance Note

Gilbert W. Joseph and Terry J. Engle (December 2005). "The Use of Control Self-Assessment by Independent Auditors". The CPA Journal. Retrieved 10 March 2012.

AICPA Operating Policies, pg. 1

Creation of the Auditing Standards Board, AICPA Operating Policies Appendix A, pg. 17, par. 2-6

Historical Background, AICPA Operating Policies Appendix A, pg. 14, par. 2-7 and pg. 15, par. 1-3

Historical Background, AICPA Operating Policies Appendix A, pg. 14, par. 4-6

Verification of Financial Statements (1929), American Institute of Accountants, Introduction, Opening Paragraph

Historical Background: Statements on Auditing Procedures; AICPA Operating Policies Appendix A; pg. 15, par. 4-7 and pg. 16, par. 1-6

Historical Background: Statements on Auditing Procedures; AICPA Operating Policies Appendix A; pg. 16, par. 7 and pg. 17, par. 1

Changes created by Sarbanes Oxley Act of 2002; AICPA Operating Policies pg. 17, par. 7 and pg. 18, par. 1

Auditing Standards Board Members, AICPA.org

Nomination of ASB Members and the ASB Chair, AICPA Operating Policies, pg. 3

Meetings of the Auditing Standards Board; AICPA Operating Policies; pg. 8, par. 1-5

Meetings of the Auditing Standards Board; AICPA Operating Policies; pg. 9, par. 1-4